# A Note to Parents

DK READERS is a compelling program for beginning readers, designed in conjunction with leading literacy experts, including Dr. Linda Gambrell, distinguished Professor of Education at Clemson University. Dr. Gambrell has served as President of the National Reading Conference, the College Reading Association, and the International Reading Association.

Beautiful illustrations and superb full-color photographs combine with engaging, easy-to-read stories to offer a fresh approach to each subject in the series. Each DK READER is guaranteed to capture a child's interest while developing his or her reading skills, general knowledge, and love of reading.

The five levels of DK READERS are aimed at different reading abilities, enabling you to choose the books that are exactly right for your child:

**Pre-level 1:** Learning to read
**Level 1:** Beginning to read
**Level 2:** Beginning to read alone
**Level 3:** Reading alone
**Level 4:** Proficient readers

The "normal" age at which a child begins to read can be anywhere from three to eight years old. Adult participation through the lower levels is very helpful for providing encouragement, discussing storylines, and sounding out unfamiliar words.

No matter which level you select, you can be sure that you are helping your child learn to read, then read to learn!

LONDON, NEW YORK, MUNICH,
MELBOURNE, and DELHI

**Author** Laura Buller
**Senior Editor** Cécile Landau
**Senior Art Editor** Ann Cannings
**Senior DTP Designer** David McDonald
**Senior Producer** Verity Powell
**Associate Publisher** Nigel Duffield

**Reading Consultant**
Deborah Lock

First American Edition, 2013

Published in the United States by DK Publishing
345 Hudson Street, New York, New York 10014

001–195198–Oct/13

DK books are available at special discounts when purchased in bulk
for sales promotions, premiums, fund-raising, or educational use.
For details, contact:
DK Publishing Special Markets
345 Hudson Street
New York, New York 10014
SpecialSales@dk.com

A catalog record for this book is available
from the Library of Congress.

ISBN: 978-1-4093-3834-5

Printed and bound in China by
L. Rex Printing Co. Ltd.

The publisher would like to thank the following for their kind
permission to reproduce their photographs:

(Key: a-above; b-below/bottom; c-centre; f-far; l-left; r-right; t-top)

**Alamy Images:** Pat Canova 16-17; Ashley Cooper 12-13,
22(background), 24-25; James Davies 10-11; David Oates
Photography 18-19; Jennie Woodcock/Bubbles Photolibrary 9.
**Corbis:** Ashley Cooper 20-21; Monalyn Gracia 14-15 (background)
Image Source; Henn Photography/Cultura 7; Gideon Mendel 5.

**Jacket images:** Front: **Corbis:** Allesfoto/Imagebroker.

All other images © Dorling Kindersley
For further information see: www.dkimages.com

Discover more at
**www.dk.com**

# Contents

# DK READERS

BEGINNING TO READ ALONE

2

# Cliffhanger!

Written by Laura Buller

DK

DK Publishing

# The Beast

Evan and Dan stood at the base of the Beast. The huge indoor climbing wall stretched all the way to the gym ceiling. Its face was dotted with climbers making their way up the wall.

"Phew," Dan whispered to his friend. "Now I see how the Beast got its name. That is one seriously tall wall."

"It's a Beast, for sure," said Evan. "but I'll bet it's a beautiful climb."

Just then, a little girl, reaching for a hold, lost her balance. She tumbled down to land on a foam crash pad. Thud! The boys rushed over to her to see if she needed help.

The girl had already scrambled to her feet when the boys arrived. She couldn't have been more than six years old.

"Hey, are you OK?" Dan asked.

"Yes, thanks, and I'm ready to tackle the Beast again," she smiled. "And win."

# At the Kit Shop

"That is the great thing about climbing," Dan said to his friend as they walked to the kit shop. "Take that girl. She isn't the biggest or strongest kid on the wall. But when she came down, she wanted to go up again."

Evan smiled. "Your hands and feet do the work, but your brain tells them where to go."

Dan clapped his buddy on the shoulder. "My brain is telling me to pick up our climbing gear and get started."

At the kit shop, Dan and Evan rented climbing shoes. The boys wriggled their toes to check for a snug fit. Sometimes climbers balance their entire weight on just one foot, so shoes are important.

The boys already had safety helmets. The last thing they needed to get was a chalk bag. Hands can get sweaty when you climb. Rubbing them on a ball of chalk keeps them dry.

# Preparing to climb

"What session have you boys picked?" asked Steve. He was a pro climber, who coached kids.

"We want to try bouldering. Climbing up with no rope sounds awesome," said Evan.

"You said it, bro. It's just your hands, your feet, and the Beast!" added Dan.

"OK, let's tick off the checklist," said Steve. "You've got helmets. You're wearing the right clothes to protect you. You're both first-aiders, right?"

"We've got the merit badges to prove it!" replied Evan.

"Go meet the Beast!" said Steve.

At the base of the Beast, Evan and Dan gave each other high fives. A small cloud of chalk dust rubbed off their hands. They were picking a path to follow.

The different routes up the wall were marked with colored holds. Some paths were easy, and others were a bit tougher.

"We've done the green level before. Let's step it up a little and try purple," suggested Evan.

The boys did a few stretches to warm up. "You know the hard part?" Dan said to his friend. "Taking the first step. It can be tricky."

"Remember when we used
to climb trees when we were
little, Dan?" his friend chuckled.
"It's just the same. Get on, and
get up. Come on, let's go!"

Up they went, finding the
first holds with their feet.
They were off.

# Boy vs Wall

One hold at a time, the boys made their way along the course. Even though they were not going up high, it was a tough challenge.

At first, the handholds and footholds were larger and close together. But soon, they were smaller and farther apart. It was much harder to keep balanced. The boys had to stretch an arm or leg way across the Beast to reach the next hold.

"Whoa!" Evan's hand slipped from the hold. He scrambled on the wall.

"Use your legs, bud!" Dan called. In their climbing lessons, the boys had been taught to rely on their legs. Legs are stronger than arms, so they can do the hard work of a climb. Arms and hands are better for balance and position.

Evan found a new hold. They were nearly at the end of the course.

At last! One final foothold, and they were there. Dan and Evan had completed the next level.

"I nearly lost it back there," said Evan. "I can't believe how hard I had to concentrate."

"That's the skill," replied Dan. "Planning each move, and then making it. Giving your head and your body a workout is why I love climbing so much."

"Do you boys love it enough to come to the canyon after school on Tuesday and join in one of our outdoor climbing sessions?" said Steve.

"Cool! That would be awesome," said Evan.

"Dan, are you in?"

"I'm in, and I'm up," laughed Dan. "I just hope I'm not going down."

# Peril on the ropes

On Tuesday, the boys met the group of climbers at Roadrunner Canyon. First, they were going to watch one of Steve's fellow instructors, Bill, demonstrate a climb. Steve told the boys that he and Bill would have time to take them bouldering later.

One end of a climbing rope was knotted to Bill's harness. The rope went through an anchor high up the canyon wall.

Steve was belaying for Bill. His job was holding the other end of the rope. As Bill climbed, Steve pulled the rope to keep it tight—and keep Bill safe.

Up Bill went! Steve adjusted the rope so there was no slack. In no time at all Bill was climbing up the steep canyon wall. Evan and Dan couldn't take their eyes off him, but when they did, they saw Steve wince in pain.

"My arm," Steve cried. "I think I've pulled something. Quick, I need help."

A young woman from the climbing group stepped forward. "Bill, come down! We've got trouble on the belay!" she cried, as she grabbed the moving rope.

"Ouch!" The rope stung her hands, but she knew she had to get control of it to get Bill down safely. Steve kept his good hand on the rope, too. Bill was coming down too quickly, but the girl hung tough. At last, she and Steve pulled the rope tight.

Bill slid down onto the crash pad. Everyone sighed in relief.

"Gosh. That was scary, but it certainly showed us the ropes," said Dan. He smiled and turned to Steve and Bill. "Ready to spot us bouldering?" he asked.

# Glossary

**Anchor**
Device, fixed to a rock or boulder, for attaching a climber's rope to

**Balanced**
Stable and in control

**Belaying**
Holding a rope tight to keep another climber safe and secure

**Bouldering**
Rock climbing without a rope

**Chalk**
White powder, used to keep hands dry when climbing

**Checklist**
List of important things to do before starting any activity

**Foothold**
Secure place to put your feet when climbing

**Gear**
Equipment used for any activity, such as climbing

**Handhold**
Secure place to grip with your hands when climbing

**Harness**
Device, worn by a climber, to attach a rope to

**Helmet**
Hard hat, worn to protect a climber's head from any falling rocks

**Holds**
Places on a climbing wall for gripping with your hands or putting your feet on —colored to tell you how difficult a path up the wall is.

**Kit**
Essential clothing and equipment

**Stretch**
Gentle exercise to warm up the muscles before any physical activity

OCT 0 7 2013